novum pro

WINFRIED SCHLOTTER

MY WORLDVIEW

THE SEARCH FOR THE TRUE AND GOOD IS THE SEARCH FOR GOD

All rights of distribution, also through movies, radio and television, photo-mechanical reproduction, sound carrier, electronic medium and reprinting in excerpts are reserved.

Printed in the European Union on eco-friendly, chlorine-free and acid-free bleached paper.

© 2019 novum publishing

ISBN 978-3-99064-606-9
Translated from German into English by Winfried Schlotter
Cover Images:
James Steidl | Dreamstime.com;
Baumann Fotostudio GmbH, Höhr-Grenzhausen
Coverdesign, Layout & Type:
novum publishing

www.novumpublishing.com

~

Since the coherences and manifestations of all sensory perceptions suggest that there is a uniform law which is inherent in all that exists, we as human beings, who are aware of our existence and think about ourselves and the world, are faced with the question of the nature of this law.

First we must recognise that all being comes into existence for us only by the information we receive through our sense organs and which becomes conscious in some way in our brain. It follows that everything perceived by people is just a reflection of the original information in the human brain. Humans, for example, perceive colours or tones, but colours and tones are only contents of consciousness of the human perception of certain information that can be interpreted in terms of their physical nature, in our example as frequencies of an electromagnetic quantum current or as an acoustic wave detectable by the sense organs such as the eye or ear. An animal perceives the same information depending on its physical state in a form that deviates more or less from human perception. Thus, all cognition is only fragmentary, and only an aspect of the whole reality is brought to our knowledge. Quantum physics even teaches us that the simultaneous determination of the position and momentum of an elementary particle is subject to an uncertainty principle and that the exact state of an object can never be determined, even with the most accurate methods of measurement. In addition, usually our terminology can only imprecisely describe what is perceptible to the senses and rationally recognisable.

Thus, if everything that we perceive and recognise is ultimately a subjective reality depending on our own form of existence, what about the real being, the objective reality? The fact that there must be an objective reality, which is independent of our own existence, we can deduce from our sensory perception of emanations from objects that can be noted by other people as existing, even if we do not have such perception ourselves, whether because we have not existed yet or because our own perception is interrupted. But that does not mean that the concerned objects, after perception ability is restored, are no longer perceptible, unless the objects themselves have meanwhile adopted a new form of existence due to objective changes.

To approach the objective reality, we need to question our observations with respect to the logic that obviously underlies all being. The physicist and philosopher Werner Heisenberg used the term "central order" for this law inherent in all things (W. Heisenberg, *Der Teil und das Ganze*). This law also determines the logical thinking of men, which, as we know, on the basis of this law is able to distinguish between true and false. The truth tolerates no contradiction in itself. If this were not the case, the opposite would be true and so this opposite should be a fundamental truth, in which manner such an assertion refutes itself.

Although as humans we do not have the possibility to perceive the real being in an objective way or to recognise it in a perfect manner, we can nevertheless, as stated above, check the subjectively perceivable for its true content, i.e. for consistency, and thus enhance our human knowledge about the objective being in the sense of truth.

Searching for the nature of the law that forms the basis of all being we encounter the concept of truth. It is consubstantial with the logic of "central order". It is, as far as we can recognise it, chronologically not changeable, i.e. of an unalterable nature.

If everything is subjected to the laws of the truth, from where comes the untruth which stands in unbridgeable contradiction to the truth? The fact that untruth and therefore contradiction and discord exist in the world, is just as evident as the truth itself and at least recognisable for logically thinking people. When asked about the nature of untruth, we must note that untruth exists as a contradiction to the truth. It does not derive its essence from the truth, but presupposes the truth. Therefore, truth is more original. It is incompatible with untruth, but the truth obviously allows contradiction, not in itself, but in that what is mutable due to freedom. For only where freedom of decision-making exists, contradiction of truth is possible. Thus, we necessarily come to the concept of freedom.

Although freedom is in contradiction to strict causality, which we initially perceive in the laws of nature, we know due to more exact physical research that this strict causality is not valid everywhere, that in the field of quantum physics various possible states coexist and probability must be applied and that causality, as we know from classical physics, only arises from the overall probability of the sum of many single events in the area of the elementary. Freedom must not be of a purely random nature, but can also mean freedom of choice. This freedom of choice highly determines the subjective feeling of a person who feels in himself the possibility to be able to decide freely between different options, although this decision may be not unmotivated and not without any reason. This self-experience of man, however, is characterised by several brain researchers and also by many psychologists as self-illusion, and they believe that they have found proof of this. Nevertheless, it must be countered that freedom must exist in some form when it comes to contradiction of the truth in what is existentially subjected to the laws of truth. Furthermore, without freedom every demand for ethical action would be an illusion, because no real alternatives would exist. Also any guilt would be unreal, because every event and action would be determined.

We therefore assume that there is one truth which is unchangeable and free of contradiction in itself, according to whose laws, as far as they are of a deterministic nature, all that is changeable happens in accordance with the one truth, but that where freedom is given, the possibility for turning away from and for contradiction of the truth also exists. The cause of the untruth and all its consequences is therefore not the truth itself, but the turning away from the truth, which is possible because of freedom.

Everything which happens in accordance with the truth is in conflict with that which is false and thus in the sense of truth is bad. As far as what is false happens consciously, freely and willingly, we speak of evil. However, good is what exists and happens in accordance with the truth. While in this case the terms *good* and *evil* are clear and definable, there is otherwise a high degree of terminology confusion. In general, as "good" is considered to be what brings the most "benefit" while "bad" or "evil" cause the most "harm", "benefit" and "harm" in different ways are brought into relation with one's own person, with parts of the whole or with the whole. Every person has therefore his own idea of values. The result is that everywhere contradictions and discord prevail. This discord is not limited to humans. Generally, every living being aspires to self-preservation, which implies on the one hand the defence against existential threat and on the other hand, as we know, the use of other organisms as a source of food, and so this behaviour leads to conflicts and deadly confrontation even in the plant world and animal kingdom.

According to the above, the question arises: what is good or bad, what is right or wrong? What can be traced back to the one indivisible truth and what is in contradiction to it? Let us assume for a moment that freedom does not exist. Then there can also be no real contradiction in the above dispute. Then all that happens can be derived from the laws of truth. Consequently, everything happens in accordance with it, no matter whether we regard it as "good" or "bad." The discord between individuals is then not a real (objective) conflict. Although there is suffering, death and destruction, these are not in contradiction to the laws of truth. However, then the question arises, why do we defend ourselves against what is supposed to be "bad" if everything happens in accordance with the truth. Is not our own (subjective) behaviour then in contradiction to the truth?

We might get the idea that there can be no freedom and therefore no dissent within the existing order in the area of inanimate nature as well as in the plant and animal world; that freedom and with it the possibility for contradiction only starts with the appearance of man.

However, we remember that according to today's physical knowledge even in inanimate nature indefiniteness, i.e. freedom, has to be taken into account.

In addition, all indications are that also the more highly developed animals are aware, similarly to humans, of the threat to and destruction of their own existence, seeing this as an evil that has to be fought. This, however, suggests that here also at least a subjective contradiction exists.

Throughout history, people have dealt with the above-mentioned problems. There is no religion which does not recognise the contradictions in the world and which does not derive consequences for the individual's own ethical action. Also, most philosophers and thinkers recognise at least the human freedom and the derivable human responsibility for right action.

If there are worldviews which deny any freedom and regard everything that happens as strictly determined, a further discussion of these is not necessary since any view that deviates from these must also be regarded as determined. However, this should not lead to contradictions according to the strict laws of a non-contradictory logic based on an indivisible truth. But if this one indivisible truth and thus the laws of logic based on it and being free of internal contradiction did not exist, all human searching for truth would also be questionable, because a reliable differentiation between what is true or false would not be possible anymore.

So we hold on to the knowledge that there is one indivisible truth, which tolerates no contradiction within itself, but that freedom exists in what is changeable, although it is existentially subjected to the laws of the truth, and that thus the possibility for turning away from the truth and so for contradiction also exists.

Therefore, the truth itself is not identical with the things which are subjected to temporal change and which have also the possibility of turning away from the truth, as far as freedom is inherent to them. In contrast to things, truth is of a purely spiritual nature.

It is recognisable for us humans only to the extent that we have the mental capacity to know the truth. The thing-like, although existentially subjected to the laws of logic and thus to truth, is not truth itself, but is obviously derived from truth. Due to its conformity to the laws of nature and due to its mutability it always has the ability to form new and complex forms, including the human being, who is even able to reflect on the origin of his own existence.

What are the reasons now, resulting from the previous insights, to take a further step and show how what we have recognised as the one indivisible truth is related to the concept of God, which we encounter in the religions, though in different notions, but as the one original creative authority? What brought the atheist and truth-seeker Edith Stein to become a convinced Christian and to say "The search for truth is the search for God"?

Although we have the help of our intellectual knowledge, without the further element of faith, access to such a personal relationship with God will presumably remain blocked to us forever. Nevertheless, important reasons speak for the fact that the original creative authority is more than a "blind natural law".

There is the question: Must the development of all creaturely life up to the human being with all his abilities not be "pre-thought"? And if all that we experience as existential is "pre-thought" by the original creative authority, did this authority then not have in itself at least the idea of all this?

This idea, which was also put forward by Plato, is quite consistent with theology, the doctrine of God. If this idea is correct, which is not provable, but is just what we think is right, it is only a short step to a personal image of God.

However, one must be careful not to humanise such an image of God. Not surprisingly it is forbidden in Judaism and Islam to make an image of God. Rightly, the early heralds of one single Creator God recognised that the faith in the gods of their neighbouring nations was a misbelief. These gods were "supernatural beings with human characteristics", far from being in line with the recognisable truth of an unitary higher reasonable being, which is the basis of everything and is beyond any human measure. But also the monotheist is in danger of aligning his image of God not with recognisable truth, but of adapting it too much to human images, whereas Buddhism in its theory of the cycle of things largely lacks the view that there must be a goal-directed creative authority, which is the basis of everything.

The Enlightenment looked for new ways to get closer to the aim of finding the truth with the help of the human mind. The natural sciences in particular have achieved significant progress up to the present. However, they have also demonstrated for the first time the fundamental impossibility of finding out the whole truth with the help of scientific methods. So we are in a dilemma. On the one hand we know that there is an objective reality and therefore also a truth and that everything that contradicts this truth leads to discord and with it to harm, but on the other hand we must realise that our human mind is not sufficient to recognise the full truth.

How should we deal with this situation? Should we confine ourselves to accepting as true only that which we can prove scientifically and irrefutably? The mathematical-scientific approach adheres largely to this strict requirement and it has been highly successful in its scientific field up to now. However, unfortunately, this science method is not sufficient to give answers to all the questions which determine our existence, thinking and action.

So we search as human beings beyond the rationally recognisable for answers, which do not exclude the possibility of error. This is especially true for the question of the right doing. In this case the mathematical-scientific way of thinking leaves us completely in the lurch. It deals not with that which should be, but with that which is, what was and what will be on the basis of logical laws. What should be is a matter of ethics and related subjects.

Thus, we come back to the points made at the beginning that there are many different value systems due to the different human worldviews, and presumably those prevail which use personal well-being as a criterion and that of the associated social group. Such a system of values is usually oriented only as far on the public welfare as this has consequences on the personal well-being and that of the own group. In contrast, the view that our activities should be guided by what serves the whole is rather a minority position. However, this position is the only one that gives hope that the conflicts and contradictions in the world can be overcome. The truth which tolerates no internal contradiction is by its nature, as far as the changeable is concerned, only then fully in line with this, if also all things that are changeable are in accordance with each other.

Seen in such a way, the search for truth is more than a question of knowledge. By searching for what truly should be the truth acquires an ethical dimension. Edith Stein, in her search for truth, considered philosophy, religion and finally arrived at Christianity. The Christian conventions were not what convinced her. Religious conventions she knew from her Jewish origin. It was the search for the really good that she had found above all in Christ and in those who were true followers of Christ. It was taking the step of faith from the intellectual knowledge of the true and good towards a personal relationship with God. What we concede to Edith Stein, of course, we must also admit to those who come to other convictions. If we recognise freedom of choice as a prerequisite for ethical action – pure epistemology gives us, as shown, not the final answer to the question of what is real, and certainly not the answer to the question of what should be – we must also accept religious freedom as part of the personal decision-making process, although we know that there can be no different truths and that contradictory views of what is and should be allow the conclusion that contradictions exist with respect to the one truth. However, the demand for religious freedom and tolerance does not mean that one must accept human error, so far as it is recognisable as such, and its consequences. The error must be counteracted by the truth. This is also valid for one's own error; i.e. any personal conviction must always be reviewed in view of the recognisable truth, and especially its ethical dimension may not be disregarded. A conviction, which, for example, considers it right to make the well-being of oneself or one's own group the standard for right action, is refutable as false, because in terms of a universal consensus of truth, i.e. freedom from contradictions, sole personal welfare or that of one's own group cannot be a measure of the welfare of the whole. Such a behaviour is no way to overcome the contradictions. As already said, only the comprehensive effort to act in accordance with the truth can overcome contradictions and conflicts.

After critical examination of this principle we find that hardly anyone can claim to meet this requirement. Everybody is too much intent on the own advantage and that of the own group. Self-preservation and preservation of one's own species and the associated desire for self-assertion and self-realisation are essential characteristics of biological evolution. We know the consequences: the more successful ones prevail. The "struggle for existence", kill or be killed, even with cunning and deceit, but on the other hand also the concern for the preservation of one's own species up to the point of self-sacrifice – all this already exists at least in the animal kingdom. However, no one would get the idea of holding plants and animals responsible for their behaviour. Their behaviour is largely genetically determined, which to a certain extent is also valid for human beings. But we humans are able to question things. "One should treat others as one would like others to treat oneself" is a golden rule which everybody can recognise as true and correct, if one knows that the other as a human individual, objectively speaking, is to be judged as no different in his needs than oneself. Here, however, the waters begin to part. While the one who follows the truth tries to act according to the principle of the golden rule, the one who uses as a guide for action only his own benefit or that of his own group shows little regard for the needs of those having no connection to him.

At this point we must ask if what we recognise as wrong is always a consequence of evil, i.e. a wrong action based on a conscious and free will choice, or is it not true that also the unconscious, on the basis of freedom, can lead to contradiction against the true and good? The possibility of a conscious, free will decision, which is the prerequisite for evil based on responsibility according to our definition, we believe can be observed in the course of evolutionary history only in humans. However, because antagonism already exists in the unconscious, animated nature, the conclusion is obvious that the false and bad are more original than evil based on responsibility, which therefore would remain limited to humans.

In most religions, however, this is seen differently. In the polytheistic religions there are gods who themselves cause evil like we humans. In the monotheistic religions these are demons, which, although originally good, have turned away from God by a free will decision and subsequently, in opposition to God, try to realise promote evil in the world. In this case, evil based on responsibility is not limited to humans, but it is existentially more original.

We are also here in the already mentioned dilemma of the deficient cognitive ability of man. If we limit ourselves to what we can recognise as proved, there is no answer to the above question, because metaphysical issues are largely beyond the human ability of cognition and related answers always depend on beliefs.

Yet it is usually not that beliefs are at the end of a fundamental epistemological discussion of the raised questions. We humans are born in a cultural and also ideological environment. Depending on their respective cultures, there are different religious beliefs that influence the thoughts and actions of people. But increasingly, modern scientific knowledge is penetrating the general awareness and superseding old ideas. As a result, there are more atheistic worldviews. However, they do not renounce ethical demands. Concerning the question of what should be, they are highly influenced by socio-political values and in this respect they are a kind of substitute for religion.

I myself was born into a Catholic family and was educated according to Christian principles. Nevertheless, I began quite early to argue with the given views. Already as a boy I asked myself the question, "Where does evil come from, if everything comes from God?" That strict laws form the basis of all physical events I learned not only at school; I could also always observe it to be true. However, this hardly helped me in the understanding of the world. When I was 15 years old my father fell seriously ill, needed long-term care and died after two years. This was a confrontation with suffering and death that moved me internally. I read Schopenhauer and found much of what I myself felt and thought confirmed by his worldview. I did not want to come to terms with death, especially the often cruel death. On the other hand, it was difficult for me to believe in the Christian resurrection and life after death. The miracle reports of the Bible did not fit my view of the strict physical laws of this world. The biblical history of creation that the first people had to die because they had sinned did not recognise the fact that man, like every animal, is subject to the law of evolution, which includes also the death of individuals and the transmission of life within the species. Death existed long before man entered the world stage. That the theory of evolution of the origin of species in principle was correct made sense to me quite early. Particularly the view that every living being and thus also human beings go again through the whole history of biological development, starting from the fertilised ovum, so to speak, in a time-lapse tempo, fascinated me. I saw evidence of it for example in the fact that frogs first exist as swimming tadpoles, or embryos of birds, instead of wings, still have hands with five fingers, i.e. that the different animal species, if one pursues their embryonic development backward, show resemblances, which get lost in the course of the development of the individual in analogy to the phylogenetic development. On the other hand, I was quite sure that the pure principle of selection had failed regarding the origin of species. The development of the whole universe, of all living things including man with his consciousness was for me due to the laws of nature and could occur only because a principle of order is inherent in the natural laws, which permits the biological development into more and more complicated forms and properties. The existence of a higher rational being which forms the basis of all and which I tried to equate with the traditional concept of God, I have never doubted. However, I had difficulties with such "truths" which were not in accordance with the scientific knowledge that could be regarded as valid.

So I looked for answers to the above issues. The "tree of knowledge", from which the first humans had eaten according to the biblical history of creation, I interpreted as the evolutionary step from animal to man. Humans, unlike animals, could distinguish "good" and "evil" and also recognise that "they had to die." Not physical death itself, but the knowledge of this death was therefore a result of the "disobedience against God", which consisted of the fact that our "human ancestors", by striving for higher cognition ability, also gained the knowledge of their own physical mortality. Also the statement of Jesus who has promised those who believe in him that they "will not see death" I interpreted similarly by applying this not to earthly death, but to the fact that one who believes in Christ and with it in the everlasting life also lives and dies in the awareness that the earthly death does not mean the end of his existence. I could live more or less with these answers, although it disturbed me that the cognition ability of man was apparently Janus-faced.

At the end of my school days such religious and philosophical questions were no longer so important for me. Friendships, my relationships with others and the relationships between people were subjects that particularly occupied me. My ideas of what should be and what I considered as possible and feasible with goodwill were very idealistic and, in retrospect, not very realistic. Thus, I have suffered from the discrepancy between what I considered as desirable and what I experienced as real. This tension was exacerbated at the beginning of my studies by separation from my family and school environment, which also had the consequence that previous friendships no longer continued in the way I had hoped. The fact that I had chosen the study of communications engineering had practical reasons. Although I was interested in the physical basis of this technology – in particular, Theoretical Electrical Engineering provided me with new insights – I was more concerned about having an assured position in later life. On the issues which really moved me, I found no answers here. These questions were rather of a philosophical and religious nature. But I had never seriously considered studying these subjects, because I feared losing the uncertain ground under my feet. So I clung to what gave me a certain security: my knowledge obtained by experience and learning and my traditional Christian faith as far as it was consistent with what I thought to be "true and good". But there was still the "contradiction" between the natural laws and the biblical miracle reports which to a large extent form the basis of Christian belief. Looking at my own existence and that of the entire cosmos as a miracle did not answer my question on this subject. All these natural wonders were in accordance with the laws of nature.

In the aforementioned miracles, if they were real events, the known laws of nature had obviously lost their validity. If God was omnipotent and thus master of the laws of nature, he was also able to annul these laws. Was that the answer? I myself had never observed that the natural laws no longer had validity. Not everything was explicable by the known laws of nature. But that was probably because we knew too little about these laws. For me, this applied particularly to the healing miracles, stigmatisations or visions, which happen up to the present day. But the biblical miracles, especially those which have been reported about Christ, could not all be interpreted in this way. For the time being my answer was that God's omnipotence was surely above the laws of nature and "that there are more things in heaven and earth than are dreamed of in our philosophy" (W. Shakespeare, Hamlet).

The moral question of what had to happen so that the world would become better and humanity could survive was more important to me. It did not really matter who was right, but that the discord between people was eliminated. Humanism, which sought international understanding and harmony between the people beyond the borders of worldviews, was what I had in mind as an ideal. But the more I strove for it, the more I had to recognise that my wishes and reality widely diverged. Even in the personal sphere I did not succeed in overcoming contradictions. Thus, I was increasingly looking for harmony with God, the true and good origin of all being. However, also here "contradictions" still existed for me. How could the "Almighty God" permit so much "terrible evil" to happen even to innocent people, especially when not caused by the people, but by the forces of nature? Was this the "punitive God", as the prophets of the Old Testament understood him?

Obviously there was an inconsistency in terms of our ideas of the "omnipotence" and the "love and mercy" of God. Did these ideas of God contain too much of human nature? Here only a sincere search for the truth could help.

If God is the truth and the origin of all being, then the laws of nature, which obey the in itself non-contradictory truth, are of divine origin too. Thus the inherent logic, which we can describe even mathematically in many areas, is by its very nature identical to the divine truth. Therefore, reports on phenomena which are contrary to these laws must be questioned. Nevertheless, care is required for a universal response.

We all know many phenomena, from which we suppose that they are in line with the natural laws, but they cannot be explained by the laws of nature so far known. There is the whole world of living beings, which obviously obeys the laws of nature, but whose behaviour is by no means always identical to that of the non-living physical world. Finally, the conscious life emerges, which hitherto has completely eluded a purely physical interpretation. Consciousness suggests a new form of existence so that our human existence appears in a light exceeding purely physical existence. The fact that *I* am in this my body, that *I* do not exist in another body as *another self*, but as *myself*, just as *other selves* have adopted existence in other bodies, is not a physical question. It rather suggests that there is something that goes beyond the purely physical.

This note is very important because it shows that the whole reality in principle cannot be revealed only with the help of scientific knowledge.

The brain scientist and Nobel laureate John Eccles describes this issue as follows:

"I believe that there is a fundamental mystery in my existence, transcending any biological account of the development of my body (including my brain) with its genetic inheritance and its evolutionary origin; and, that being so, I must believe similarly for each one of you and for every human being. And just as I cannot give a scientific account for my origin – I woke up in life, as it were, to find myself existing as an embodied self with this body and brain – so I cannot believe that this wonderful gift of a conscious existence has no further future, no possibility of another existence under some other unimaginable conditions" (Eccles, John C., Facing Reality, Springer-Verlag New York/Heidelberg/Berlin 1970, science library, p. 83).

"Transcending the physical (metaphysical, i.e. 'beyond the physical')" therefore means that not everything can be disclosed by a physical explanation or interpretation. In other words, there is obviously something still more fundamental than the rationally accessible physical world and its laws, which are only partial aspects of the divine truth inherent in all. However, this does not imply that in the area of metaphysics logic is discarded and arbitrariness prevails. The cognition that a consistent logic is inherent in all being is so evident that we must assume that also the metaphysical is subject to the divine truth which underlies all. This is valid both in terms of the phenomenon of "miracles", which cannot be excluded, and in terms of our understanding of the "omnipotence of God", which cannot be arbitrary and contradictory. God does nothing that contradicts his own being, i.e. the truth.

"Miracles" are therefore phenomena that are very well in accordance with the fundamental truth, but they cannot be interpreted only physically, because they are based on a more original and deeper underlying logic.

After what has been said about the immutability of the divine truth, however, the question remains: What about "the love and mercy of God"?

We humans repeatedly have the experience that true love prevails where there is harmony with the true and good. Therefore, love also has a divine nature. However, we humans also are seeking "love" where it is not the harmony with the true and good that is in the foreground, but the feeling of happiness which results from the harmony of our *Self* with the *You* or more in general from a relationship with persons or objects of our appreciation. With regard to what we call "love", it is similar to what we regard as "good". We are not guided by what is objectively true and good, but by subjective preferences. That is why we find it so difficult to love in all situations God who alone is invariably true and good. And also the love for others is often not oriented towards what is truly good, but towards what we like. Divine love, however, is only focused on what is true and good. This also applies to the "mercy of God", which consists of the fact that wherever there is freedom, the possibility for returning to the true and good also exists. "Love and mercy of God" and thus salvation and redemption are therefore always effective where we try to live and to act in accordance with the true and good, i.e. in obedience to God, which also includes in particular to endure suffering. However, the "love and mercy of God" are not a measure of the fulfilment of our wishes. This also explains why much of what we perceive as "evil" in reality happens in accordance with the divine truth. But the contradiction to this truth, i.e. the rebellion against God, leads to the fact that we question the "love and mercy of God".

In general, the question arises: What about that which we subjectively experience as "good"? To what extent are for example "beauty" and "happiness" of a divine nature? To answer these questions I have to come back to what I said about the "good". If we define the good as all that is in line with the one indivisible truth, so everything which is objectively good is included. However, beauty, happiness and other aspects of what we feel to be "good" are not always aspects of the true and good. The problem is that even the false and the evil use these aspects. Deceptions and false allurements consist in the fact that we make a positive impression the standard for our actions, detached from what is truly good, which, however, often leads to evil, as we know. But this does not mean that beauty and happiness are not desirable in themselves. In particular in the perfect harmony with the true and good we experience beauty and happiness in a special way. So they are also of divine origin. Only their abuse has evil results, like everything that exists and turns away from the true and good. The same is valid, by the way, especially for human sexuality.

Realising that the true and good alone must be the guiding principle of our actions revealed to me a new vision of the redemption of our world full of contradictions:

If freedom is a characteristic feature of divine truth, God admits sin, i.e. the turning away from him, and thus also the evil within his creation resulting from the conflict with the truth, but where conversion to the true and good happens, healing and redemption happen too. Because truth and falsehood, good and evil are, according to their contradictory nature, in constant conflict with each other, ultimately perfect redemption happens only after turning away from the false and the evil to the true and good or after complete and final separation of the true from the false and the good from all evil. Therefore, the overcoming of all contradictions will only occur at the end of the redemptive path and only a creation which is in line with the divine truth can fully experience God's saving power.

Thus the Christian doctrine of salvation became understandable as well. Only the absolute obedience to God, or in other words the unlimited love of the divine truth and thus the ending of the contradictions within creation, could provide salvation. The way of salvation shown by Christ, followed in absolute obedience to God even as far as martyrdom, was the true path that could bring salvation.

But obedience to God presupposes not only the unlimited love of God, but also the ability to recognise the true and good, which is not sufficiently given to us human beings solely by our intellect. If God is the origin of all being and we are his creatures, then a dialogical relationship should exist between Him and us, which however can be interrupted by sin and guilt. But on the other hand it can be re-established by faith in Him as our Creator and especially by listening to one's personal conscience, the divine compass in us, which is in line with the true and good. This listening and this dialogue are by their very nature real prayer. However, by praying for the fulfilment of personal wishes without listening to the will of God and without searching for His divine truth the healing strength of the true prayer can hardly become effective. However, our conscience is no guarantee that we will not go astray. One can quieten the conscience, even silence it. By false convictions or temptations, but also by the fear of suffering and death we are always in danger of leaving the path of truth and the truly good. But just as a good navigator never loses sight of the destination, but always finds a way to it, so it is with us when our conscience and thus our measure of right thinking and acting is based on the eternally true and good ground of all being, namely God, who can be experienced by reason and faith.

Thus the rational-related cognitive abilities of man had a high priority for me in the search for the truth. But also the Christian faith acquired a new meaning for me, mainly because of the way of salvation shown by Christ for overcoming sin and its consequences. Though there were still many things in the past and present of Christianity which caused annoyances, these were the wrongness that is inherent more or less in everything that needs salvation. The history of salvation, which began with the search of man for the true and good, was a long path that did not end with Christ, but in its now perfect focus on God's love and charity gives the best hope of healing. People who have gone this way are witnesses of it. The love for God and the charity of St. Francis of Assisi went so far that he endured suffering and privation like Christ and included all creation in his compassionate love. Countless others who tried to follow Christ, took care of the needy, sick and dying people in unselfish love. Also there have always been Christians who have raised courageously the voice of truth and justice at times of injustice and suppression, even by offering their lives.

But, on the other hand, does this mean that other doctrines and beliefs are wrong? The idea of salvation does not exclude anyone from the outset. "Who we are before God is really who and what we are: nothing more and nothing less!" This is the convincing judgement of Francis of Assisi. All who are of good will may attain salvation, whose goal is the perfect realisation of the true and good. Hence, everyone is to be measured according to the extent to which the realisation of the true and good guides his thinking and acting. In a negative sense this is also true for those who refer to Christ, but in truth do evil. The wrong and the bad cannot participate in a redeemed world. Perfect redemption from all evil then also means that there can be no more disagreement on the question of the true and good, and that all recognising and acting will happen in perfect harmony with the divine truth.

On the other hand, if falsehood and wickedness have no place in a redeemed world, the separation from God and his kingdom, eschatologically seen, must be final for that part of creation which refuses to return to the true and good. The religions use the term "hell" for this, which, however, is strongly influenced by mythological images. Because the future is largely unknown to us, there remains only the possibility for us to draw conclusions from our past and present experiences as regards what a life full of falsehood and malice might look like. We know about the consequences of hypocrisy, unkindness and hate up to deadly use of violence, which reach their climax in brutal armed conflicts. We even sometimes use the term "hell" for this, although the proper meaning of the term "hell" is that this state is final, i.e. unlimited and therefore eternal. Thus, the consequences of evil are known to us in principle. However, a concretisation of our imagination about what we call "hell" in the eschatological sense should be avoided because of our defective knowledge and the danger of misbelief.

Similarly, but with a reverse meaning, we use the term "heaven", which represents the status of a creation liberated from all evil in the "kingdom of God". Here we know that this redeemed part of creation will no longer suffer from any evil since its causes will be overcome.

Important in this context is the statement that the future of the world is not irrelevant for our personal existence. The view that for a person as a conscious *self* there will be no more life after death is questionable, because the conditions for the life of every human being as a conscious *self* before and after its existence, i.e. before conception and after the death of the respective person, are not significantly different. The probability that I exist today as a conscious *self* is in principle the same in comparison to a future existence of this *self* in another form of existence, if I assess it from the perspective before my current existence.

The origin of all being, which is recognisable for our mind as the unique indivisible truth and which we experience by faith also as personal God who has created each of us with a unique existence as a *self* in a given body in space and time, also has the power to let this *self* take a new existence in other form and under other conditions. Depending on one's belief, here concepts appear such as immortality of the soul, resurrection, reincarnation, transmigration of the soul. These concepts are different faith-dependent paraphrases of the common view that our *self* has a future after its present form of existence.

What this future will really look like is beyond our knowledge. While in Judaism a strong belief in the bodily resurrection of the dead at the end of this world characterises its idea, in Christianity the immortality of the soul is more in the foreground, in which one understands the non-physical portion of a person, "the real *self*". The idea common to both religions that this *self* "on the Day of Judgement" will assume a new physical form is quite closely related to the Buddhist-Hindu idea of reincarnation. However, "reincarnation" and "transmigration of the soul" have no eschatological orientation in these religions, and the identity of a person, i.e. of the *self*, is seen differently, that is to say, "reincarnation" means a new life in a different physical body, as another individual.

For Christians the belief in "the bodily resurrection of Christ" is also of central importance, because in the gospels, while naming credible witnesses, concrete statements are made about "manifestations of the Risen", which indicate a completely new form of existence. Because here, knowledge-based access on the basis of the laws known to us is totally impossible, for the believer, for whom the truth must be self-consistent, the statement already made with respect to the "miracles" remains valid, i.e. there must exist a more fundamental, "transcendent reality" beyond the physical laws known to us.

After the basic issues have been addressed, I want, as someone who gives high priority to the scientific knowledge for the sake of truth and who tries at the same time to reconcile the religious dimension of the human being with the recognisable truth, to deal in more detail with the questions which in my view need critical consideration. As already explained at the beginning, no one is in possession of the whole truth and errors cannot be excluded, especially where human cognition has its limits. Because religious convictions are largely beyond the possibility of cognitive, scientific verification, religious antagonisms are particularly difficult to overcome. Therefore, when tolerance is missing, conflicts are inevitable. The persecution of believers of other religions up to their physical destruction is historical reality and continues today.

I hold no brief for relativism. I am convinced that there is only one objective truth. But we must always be aware that our knowledge is imperfect and that we depend on beliefs as guidelines for our actions. This is why mutual tolerance has to be demanded in favour of our own convictions and also for the sake of truth. Where clear errors exist, however, these should be named as such. Thus, for example, we know that in the four gospels divergent statements are made. Although when considered on their own these are not of serious importance, it follows that these texts, which are regarded as the basis of faith, are not free of defects. Similar reasoning applies to doctrines represented in the history of the church and later corrected on the basis of scientific knowledge. To make such mistakes and to err is human. However, the resulting prosecutions and convictions of innocent people represent a burden of guilt and sin, which can hardly be eliminated. Before now in the Jewish religious history too, intolerance and wrong religious zeal played an inglorious role. Also the militant Islam citing the Koran, the "holy book of Islam", is largely intolerant towards other faiths. Already a simple comparison of the "holy books" of the world religions Judaism, Christianity and Islam shows us that they cannot all be equally "divine revelation". Given that there can be only one self-consistent objective truth, contradictory statements about what is "true" and "good" should therefore be questioned. As far as these texts credibly give evidence of what is true and good in terms of a critical search for the truth, they are important healing sources on the way to the salvation of the world. However, making them without restriction in each case the absolute measure for what is true and good is religious fundamentalism that does not overcome possible errors and their consequences.

Nevertheless, this does not mean that one must renounce a religious belief and thus a religious community. Even the apostle Peter convincingly answered Jesus' question "Will you also go away?": "Lord, to whom shall we go? You have the words of eternal life. And we believe and are sure that You are the Christ, the Son of the living God" (John 6, 67–69). The disciples of Jesus who were in search of the true and good had to decide. Recognising and believing are the key conditions for human acting determined by the search for the true and good. Where cognition and belief are not contradictory but complementary, all conditions for responsible decision of conscience are fulfilled. However, out of this no justifications can be derived for intolerance towards other religious and ideological convictions deviating from one's own view.

But we have to deal with the issue of tolerance in a little more detail. As I explained above, everything that does not correspond to the truth is not good. Accordingly, also errors are bad. Where you can recognise the error and identify it as such, you have to counteract it and try to overcome it with the help of the truth. The situation is different with regard to tolerance towards the erring person, since the error is not based on malice, but on the lack of knowledge, which is more or less characteristic of all humans. Therefore, the basic principle is that tolerance has to be practised towards all people of goodwill, regardless of whether they are wrong. The legal system must ensure that the rights and freedoms of all, even those with opposing views are adequately taken into account. However, they are to be limited where the rights of others are violated. Here therefore the tolerance ends; that is, also in a pluralistic society there must be limits of action. The laws to be created for this purpose ideally must be guided by the principle already stated: "You should not be allowed to treat others in a way that you would not like to be treated by others."

But regarding the tolerance question also the case must be considered that we are dealing not with error, but with malice. It is obvious that the principle of tolerance cannot be equally valid in this case. Who consciously and voluntarily does what is recognisably wrong and bad, must expect sanctions. However, the penal legislation is a difficult metier and contains the potential danger that further injustice is caused by it. Hence, the prohibition of people taking the law into their own hands is correct. But also the judiciary, which should ensure the enforcement of right and law as an independent authority between delinquent persons and victims, is not always capable to fulfil this function. Firstly, there is the legislation itself, which is largely based on state and societal interests rather than asking what is right or wrong in the sense of the true and good; on the other hand it is hardly possible to clarify all the facts of a penal matter so that the question of personal guilt can always be clearly decided. Above all, the question of the extent of personal guilt, in view of the fact that human action is largely conditioned, can hardly be answered. Hence, the legal certainty and the protection of victims must be in the foreground in all legal cases, while the actual punishment of the culprit should be subordinated to this objective. For the same reasons, the death penalty should generally be rejected as means of justice.

In this context a little on the subject of international law should be said. Conflicts between nations should be assessed similarly to conflicts between individuals, but whereas in the latter case usually the respective national legal authorities are responsible for the legislation and the law enforcement, in many areas of international coexistence we do not have supranational legal authorities and particularly those which have the possibility to enforce the necessary international law, where it exists and is disregarded. Especially in armed conflicts, doors and gates are opened for state arbitrariness, usually under the pretext of the "right of self-defence", but sometimes also under the pretext of a "justified intervention". However, there is certainly a right of self-defence and within narrow limits also a right of intervention for the world community of states. This in particular means the right to protect the citizens of a state against unjustified external and internal violence. Because the state has the task of ensuring the welfare of its citizens, one can deduce from this that there exists not only the right but also the obligation of the state to protect its citizens. This implies in turn that there is also a civic duty for the individual citizens to make a personal contribution to the protection of the state community. On the other hand, the world community of states also has an obligation to secure world peace and has a joint responsibility for the security of peoples and ethnic groups whose right to exist is threatened.

But how should the individual citizen behave if the state itself acts against the international law and requires this from its citizens, too? Here what was ascertained, when discussing how contradictions and conflicts can be overcome, is still valid. Human action must be based on what is true and good. Finally, how to meet this requirement is a matter of conscience for the individual person. The same applies even if the state is acting on a legal basis, where the laws themselves do not meet the requirement to be based on what is true and good. In all these cases we rely on our consciences. One's conscience, after careful examination of the question of what most likely meets the true and good, can be the only guideline for responsible and ethical acting, even if it is not always free from error.

I will not and cannot look at all cases where we are in moral conflict. Even everyday situations often cause problems for us. Here, however, it appears that the one whose conscience is characterised by a personal relationship with God is left less alone. Especially in listening to God as the origin of all that is true and good, we learn best what is good and right and obtain through faith in Him the help to do what we have recognised as good and right.

Based on what has been said it is necessary to deal with further conclusions. First there is the commitment to the love of truth, which is a prerequisite for what is good. However, we know that the truth can be also hurtful and destructive. Here the question arises, what is hurt or destroyed? Ultimately, it is the false that is often painfully destroyed by the truth. But also evil makes use of the truth and it abuses knowledge and cognition in order to satisfy its bad intentions. Therefore, one must cautiously deal with the truth, but without sinning against it and against what is good in truth. There is also another danger posed by an unconditional search for knowledge. So today's scientific research should not be assessed only as positive. Often it is conducted without regard for the welfare of others and of the whole. The search for knowledge and cognition can also be presumptuous. We recall here the "forbidden fruit from the Tree of Knowledge", which promised "equality with God" (Gen.3, 5).

As you can see, even when we are dealing with the truth, we come to the earlier statement that scientific knowledge alone does not provide a binding guideline for ethical conduct. Accordance with the truth always requires that you are in accordance with the origin of all that is true and good, namely God. Without the step of faith towards this personal relationship with God we are left alone, not only in the question of what is good and right to do, but without listening to God, who indeed is the source of all our knowledge and experience of what is true and good, there is also little hope that we will ever achieve the goal of a world without discord and contradictions in spite of all our knowledge and our striving for cognition.

While the handling of truth is not without problems, this also applies to dealing with freedom to an even greater extent. Although freedom as part of the truth is good in itself, it is also a precondition for the turning away from the truth and thus for all that is wrong and bad. It is not for us to judge about the fact that this is so.

As far as we have freedom, we know that the possibility and with it also the responsibility is given to us to select from different action alternatives. The person who understands freedom in such a way that out of this a moral entitlement also arises, to act within the scope of the given possibilities according to one's own wishes, creates a contradiction between what is true and good and what on the basis of freedom can be reversed. However, from this contradiction results all discord and all evil, as we know. Self-responsible acting which turns to God, the origin of all that is true and good, on the contrary leads to the overcoming of evil and even gives dignity to the person acting in freedom. But obedience to God also means that all that remains to be done is what has been recognised as the right thing to do. However, does this not also mean loss of freedom? At this point we need to look a bit more closely at the term "freedom". We have understood the term "freedom" as the opposite of "determinism" within what is changeable. In the field of conscious human activity this leads to the "freedom of choice", which presupposes for its part that alternatives of action exist. These are often themselves conceptually equated with "freedom". However, in our approach this causes misunderstandings. "Freedom" in our sense is always a "non-deterministic process", while the existing alternatives must be considered as "degrees of freedom". But this does not imply that their presence is always combined with "freedom", i.e. "a non-deterministic process". So for example, a cube has six degrees of freedom that are statistically equi-probable. However, the result of a dice roll is not undetermined; with full knowledge of the boundary conditions in the sense of classical mechanics it is quite determinable. The situation is similar to the formation of various types of electromagnetic waves in waveguides. The boundary conditions "decide" which wave type from the number of possible types of waves is actually formed.

In humans, there are the motives that normally determine which alternatives – these correspond to the "degrees of freedom" – we choose. As far as this decision-making process is completely determined, we cannot speak of "freedom of choice". Freedom in our sense means that we can "freely" decide in spite of all motives for one or another possible action alternative.

Therefore, the fact that one can always choose only one from several existing alternatives does not mean a loss of freedom. However, it is true that the degree of freedom or the area of freedom is increasingly restricted by a reduction of the possible action alternatives, until finally with loss of any area of freedom no more freedom is given.

But what do things look like in practice? Often freedom of action does not mean that one has the possibility to decide between the true and good on the one hand or the false and bad on the other hand. True and false, good and bad are mostly interwoven with each other. Sometimes you have only the choice between several evils. In all these cases it only remains for us to choose, after careful consideration and in obedience to God, what is better or less evil. This can also mean "not acting", which strictly speaking is also an "action alternative".

An important aspect of freedom has yet to be mentioned. Those who have influence and exercise power often decide on the areas of freedom of other people. So for example, the legislator determines scopes for action whereby transgressions are penalised. Particularly despots try to impose their own will on others. But also those who feel committed to truth and goodness are convinced that areas of freedom must be limited in case of possible abuse. Liberalism, however, relies to a large extent on the personal responsibility of individuals even if that implies accepting abuse. What points of orientation do we have here?

If we use again the true and good as a measure, whereby freedom is good in itself, but its abuse is an evil, we must grant areas of freedom at least there, where responsibility is given. Preventing abuse by restricting freedoms is not in the spirit of freedom. On the other hand, one cannot simply allow the abuse of freedom. What remains, if you do not want to restrict freedom but to combat its abuse, is on the one hand conscience training and strengthening of the sense of responsibility, and on the other hand the repression of abuse of freedom by punishment on a legal basis. However, both presuppose that autonomous action is possible. Therefore, the humane criminal law does not allow the criminal conviction of children and recognises only a limited criminal responsibility of adolescents. But where no personal responsibility is given, there remains only the vicarious takeover of the responsibility by others and, if this is not possible, only the restriction of freedoms; if otherwise, dire consequences are to be feared.

In this context I remember a class excursion to Berlin, where my classmate Hans-Georg Heer and I as 18-year-olds left our group after attending the international soccer game of Germany against Austria, and we did not appear as agreed at the Deutsche Oper in East Berlin. The next day, both of us were put under house arrest in our youth hostel and had to write an essay on the topic: "How much freedom may one permit to a young person of your educational level?"

I do not remember how I dealt with this question, but I was aware that we had not acted correctly and the penalty was justified. Only in later years did I realise what possible consequences there could have been in the case of adversity resulting from our behaviour, above all for the teaching staff entrusted with the supervision. Undoubtedly, neither our sense of responsibility was sufficiently sharpened despite our 18 years nor the related "personal responsibility" according to today's legal opinion, because from an ethical point of view there is certainly no "full personal responsibility" in the sense that you can overlook all consequences of your actions.

Due to the inherited and environment-related influences the measure of our actions is furthermore less based on what is recognisable as good and right, but on what determines our subjective values. This is also the reason that this matter cannot be dealt with without legislation. Even "mature citizens" may need guidance and must, if necessary, be withheld from doing "evil" by threatening and enforcing sanctions. What here is regarded as "evil" is specified by the legislature and may not always be congruent with what is objectively seen as evil. Any legislation and jurisdiction is ultimately the acknowledgement that the sense of responsibility of the individual is not sufficient to adequately ensure togetherness within a society.

The right degree of personal freedom must therefore be based on the level of actual sense of responsibility of a person. Nevertheless, the state legislation cannot do justice to that principle, because it neither knows the individual circumstances of each individual nor has practicable methods to meet the needs of every individual by a differentiated consideration.

The ideal thus remains the education of the people to acquire more self-responsibility, and where this is not possible, the regulation of freedom rights by the legislation and judiciary, whereby the legal organs themselves are committed to the laws and these in turn must be consistent with what is recognisable as true and good. For the individual person, however, in view of the fact that the ideal and reality mostly diverge, one's own decision of conscience which must also be in line with what is recognisable as true and good, and for those who believe in God the guidance by Him as the last authority of all true and good, is relevant for all personal, liberal acting.

Although "good" is definable as in accordance with the truth and as such is also experienced, we must be careful concerning what we commonly regard as "truly good". "No one is good but God alone" Jesus says to a young man who calls him "good master" (Mark 10, 17–18). At first sight this statement seems incomprehensible and contradictory, because in the Biblical Creation Report it is explicitly emphasised that God regarded his creation as "good" too, which is reasonable because everything derived from the truth and therefore initially consistent with it must be regarded as good. However, as initially discussed, we know that creation no longer conforms totally with what is derived only from the truth, but that it has become imperfect by turning away from the truth. Therefore, the statement that "God alone is good" means nothing else than "God alone is perfect", or conversely the whole creation is "affected" by the loss of perfection.

When Jesus says "God alone is good," he wants to stress that we have only to act according to God in order to do good. Final deliverance from what is not good, therefore only happens when one is in complete accordance with God. This in turn presupposes that one believes in the true God and can recognise the will of God. Jesus even goes a step further, saying: "No one comes to the Father except through me" (John 14, 6). This means that we can only recognise the true God and his will, when we look at Jesus, trust in him and follow his instructions. Under these conditions is the assertion still correct that all people who are of good will are chosen for salvation and that everybody has to be assessed according to the extent to which the realisation of the true and good is a guideline of his thinking and acting?

If we describe the striving for what is true and good as "good will", all those who are of "good will" are well on the way to what is the origin of all true and good. For the believing Christian this is God who reveals himself in his creation so far as it is in harmony with its Creator, in the faith in Jesus Christ and by the Spirit of Truth. This path can still be very long; it even can lead occasionally in the wrong direction, but the so-seeker is oriented over and over again towards what he can recognise as true and good. He will therefore progress in this cognitive process.

According to the Christian understanding of salvation the faith in God, and according to the statement of Jesus, with it also the belief in him are preconditions for the world's salvation. The question of whether and how an individual person takes part in this salvation can hardly be answered from a cognitive view. Here again we are dependent on faith and trust. Christ speaks of himself as the judge of the world, who will separate the good from the bad, even after the death of an individual. Therefore, all who are good might share in a redeemed world, for which reason also those of "good will" may hope for salvation.

The situation is different when we do not strive for what is "truly good", but our effort is primarily directed at making our life "comfortable". Then it is self-love, not love for the true and good or love for the neighbour that determines our actions. According to the Christian understanding of salvation such behaviour leads further away from God and only an inner conversion can lead to salvation. But even our ability of cognition being based on our rational mind tells us that salvation of the world and therefore also our own salvation is not possible in this way.

"God alone is good" thus also means that only the pursuit of the true and good, which for the one who believes in God is realised in the love of God and thereby also in the love of neighbour, leads to salvation.

In everything we do, whether it be the search for the truth, our use of freedom, or our striving for the good, there remain for us in view of our limited ability of cognition only the faith in God and the loving obedience to what we can recognise as true and good and thus as the will of God.

However, in our honest efforts for the true and good we have to deal once again with the claim of Jesus that the redemption of the world and thus our own salvation is not possible without him. For this purpose it is necessary to answer the question: "Who do we believe is Jesus?"

Because we ourselves were not his companions, we are dependent on the testimony of those who met him during his life on this earth. Many words and deeds of Jesus were written down at an early stage and have been handed down to us. There are above all the statements which Jesus made about himself. Particularly in John's Gospel Jesus clearly talks about himself as the Messiah and the son sent by God, who does the works of his Father in order to save and ultimately judge the world. On the demand of his critics to tell them, whether he is the Messiah, he answers: "I told you, but you believed not. The works that I do in my Father's name they bear witness of me" (John 10, 25). And furthermore he says of himself: "I and my Father are one" (John, 10, 30). And elsewhere: "He that honours not the Son honours not the Father which has sent him" (John 5, 23).

Among his disciples, above all were Andrew and his brother Simon, who at an early stage professed Jesus as the Messiah sent by God, as the Christ, i.e. the anointed of God. Thus, Andrew leads his brother to Jesus and says to him: "We have found the Messiah" (John 1, 41).

On the question of Jesus "But whom say you that I am?" Simon answers: "You are the Christ, the Son of the living God." To which Jesus replies: "Blessed are you, Simon, son of Jonas. For flesh and blood have not revealed this to you, but my Father which is in heaven" (Matt. 16, 17).

If we do not question the content of these gospel reports, we must take note that Jesus sees himself as the Messiah predicted by the prophets, as the Christ, the son of God, who is sent by God as a rescuer and saviour to mankind. For his legitimisation he refers to the works he does according to his divine mission. When John the Baptist sends two of his disciples to Jesus to ask him: "Are you he who should come, or should we wait for another", Jesus gives them the answer: "Go and report to John what you have seen and heard: The blind receive their sight and the lame walk, the lepers are cleansed and the deaf hear, the dead are raised up and the poor have the gospel preached to them and blessed is he, whosoever shall not be offended in me" (Matt. 11, 2–6).

To those who take offence at his divine claim, he says: "If I do not the works of my Father, you do not believe me. But if I do and you will believe not me, believe the works that you may know and understand that the Father is in me and I am in the Father" (John 10, 37–38).

Concerning the works of Jesus we are also dependent on the testimony of others, because we have not been eyewitnesses. However, the miracles of Jesus are causing for us, today's "enlightened" people, as explained above, problems of faith, because they stand in certain "contradiction" with our scientific knowledge. On the other hand, there is the testimony of the disciples of Jesus and especially of his mother Mary that has been handed down to us as historically credible. In particular, those who as Jesus' companions heard his words directly and saw his actions have proved their credibility almost without exception being witnesses and martyrs in life and death. Even if we assume that not everything reported in the gospels about Jesus accurately reproduces in a scientific sense what happened, we must admit after an honest assessment that the work of Jesus exceeded every human dimension. The statement that Jesus was responsible for many "signs and wonders" cannot be dismissed as implausible simply by pointing to an existing "contradiction" to the scientific knowledge we have today, in particular, since we must assume, as explained above, that there must exist an even more basic metaphysical reality beyond the physical laws known to us.

When Jesus refers to the works that he accomplishes in accord with the divine mission, then he wants to make clear that they are not man-made or devil's work, as his adversaries try to interpret them, but that God, the origin of all that is true and good, causes them through him as the God-sent Redeemer. Thus the belief in the miracles of Jesus is an important prerequisite for the belief in his divine legitimisation and with it also in his work of redemption. When Jesus calls himself the Saviour and also the judge of the world, this is a claim that exceeds everything that others have proclaimed as prophets and messengers of salvation.

When we look back at the history of mankind, the first important prophets who claimed divine inspiration in receiving personal revelations from the one Creator God appear in the history of the people of Israel. The biblical traditions of the Old Testament report on this as follows:

Beginning with Abraham, to whom the promise is given to be the progenitor of a great nation, which manifests itself in the 12 tribes of Israel through Isaac, Jacob and his 12 sons, there emerges among this people during his exile in Egypt a religious leader in the person of Moses, to whom YHWH, the God of Israel, reveals himself personally in the burning bush and asks him to lead his people from the slavery in Egypt into the "promised land". On Mount Sinai Moses receives from God the tablets of the law with the 10 commandments, which afterwards were stored in the sanctuary of the Ark of the Covenant, thenceforth embodying God's covenant with his people. The Torah – the five books of Moses – which are also considered as divine revelation, have always formed the religious basis of Judaism. Later, there are above all the prophets of Israel who carry on the hope for redemption first of their own people, but also others. They are the messengers of the promise that from the tribe of Judah the Messiah will come, the servant sent by God, to save his people.

The mentioned religious leaders of Israel saw themselves indeed as messengers of divine revelation and their divine legitimisation is also underpinned in the biblical reports by signs and miracles, but they saw themselves only as admonishers and as messengers of divine promises, while Christ said of himself that through him the fulfilment of the promises had come. The fact that many people took offence at this is convincingly demonstrated in the gospel reports. "Is he not the carpenter's son?" ask the ones who know his family environment and "He blasphemes against God" say the others to whom, as teachers of the scriptures, the claim of Jesus to be the Christ, the son of God, seems a diabolical arrogance. Only those who have experienced Jesus' mercy and love for the poor, sick, outcasts and repentant sinners and believe in the divine power of his miracles, recognise him as the Messiah foretold by the prophets.

Paul, who changes from being a devout Jewish observer of the religious law and from a pursuer of Christians into a convinced follower of the teaching of Jesus, subsequently becomes the worldwide messenger and teacher of the faith in Jesus Christ, together with the disciples of Jesus. Also Paul must be seen like the prophets of the Old Testament as a herald of the faith in salvation, which emerged in Israel and continues in terms of the salvific history without any break, but now based on faith in Jesus Christ as the promised and incarnate saviour of the world.

In contrast, as indicated below, we encounter the figure of the prophet Muhammad who by the proclamation of his revelations written down in the 114 suras of the Quran became the founder of the Islamic world religion. Although his teachings contain numerous references to Jewish and Christian roots, nevertheless he is not in the tradition of the biblical doctrine of salvation. Even though he acknowledges important biblical persons, including Jesus, as early representatives of the one God, he claims that only he proclaims the true message of salvation, which was revealed to him by God in a perfect manner, but without seeing himself as the promised and expected Messiah according to the Bible. Unlike Jesus, he believes that it is justified for the defence of his followers and for the true doctrine to use force and if necessary to take up arms.

From a critical viewpoint we have to realise that divine revelation, even if it takes place at different times and in different forms, can always occur only in the form of the one indivisible truth. Contradictory divine truths cannot exist. Therefore we have to review all proclaimed "divine revelations" for consistency and credibility. Initially it can be said that most messengers of salvation, as far as we can assess it, were themselves convinced of the rightness of their mission. This is therefore not a sufficient criterion for the proclamation of the truth. From our own experience we know that we can be wrong, even if we act in "good faith".

When looking back to Moses and the prophets of Israel, we see from today's perspective that the absolute attachment to the letter of the Mosaic law and the religious intolerance, as well as the idea that the military victories and defeats of the people of Israel or even the personal welfare or misfortune of individuals are direct consequences of godliness or sins respectively of the people or the person concerned, are not in line with our conceptions which on the one hand are influenced by Christianity, but on the other hand also strengthened by rational considerations.

The situation is similar relating to the valuation of the religious rules and the assessment of religious and ideological tolerance in Islam. But Christianity, too, knows an overvaluation of religious conventions, and religious and ideological intolerance has characterised the confrontation with dissenters also in Christianity for centuries. However, it would be wrong to blame Jesus and his doctrine of salvation for it. Jesus was indeed strict in his judgement of all evil, but despite all his efforts for the salvation of mankind he respected the freedom and personal responsibility of individuals, and rejected violence as a means of enforcement and defence of his teaching. On the contrary, by bearing the cross and by suffering for the sake of the true and good he showed us the way to overcome evil and to find the path to salvation.

In the ranking behind Christianity and Islam, Hinduism, followed by about 13% of the world's population, is the third largest religion of the world. It has its origins in India and consists strictly speaking of different religious beliefs and practices, whose followers were given the collective name of Hindus to distinguish them from Christians, Muslims, Buddhists and Jews. However, there is neither a uniform doctrine of faith, nor a central institution that can speak for all Hindus. Among Hindus, even the ideas of God and views on life, death and salvation are very different. But there is the common idea of rebirth by reincarnation, which is why in India Buddhism is regarded as a Hindu doctrine, too.

Thus, Buddhism also has its origins in India. About five centuries before Christ, Siddhartha Gautama (Buddha) had already proclaimed his doctrine, which today, as Buddhism, is the fourth largest religion in the world. Even Buddha had a sort of revelation, i.e. an inner enlightenment, which led him to gain insights and to the way to overcome suffering in the world. The result was a Buddhist practice which is essentially based on the "Four Noble Truths", firstly, recognising that life is marked by suffering, secondly, that this suffering is caused by three mental poisons, namely "greed", "hate" (also interpretable as the search for "self-assertion of an illusionary self towards the fellow beings") and "blindness" or "ignorance" (also interpretable as the opposite of "wisdom"), thirdly, that the suffering can be stopped by eliminating these causes, and that fourthly this way of salvation is achieved through the "Eightfold Path". This "Eightfold Path" is divided into eight virtues that can be described as follows: 1. right view; 2. right intention; 3. right speech; 4. right conduct; 5. right livelihood; 6. right effort; 7. right mindfulness; 8. right meditation.

Like the Hindus, the Buddhists also believe that every living being is subject to a cycle of birth and rebirth. The aim of the Buddhist doctrine of salvation is to overcome this cycle and to reach the state of "Nirvana" through the practice of virtues and through the acquiring the right insight. "Nirvana" is unlike "heaven" in the monotheistic religions. It is not a "divine place of eternal bliss", but rather a "state of detachment" from an otherwise endless cycle of suffering and imperfection. The main differences of Buddhism compared with Judaism, Christianity and Islam, however, are a missing focus on a personal Creator God, from whom everything emanates and to whom everything is subjected, as well as a different conception of the personality of the individual which is not seen as a distinctive uniqueness. All in all, Buddhism is a belief that has a high degree of ethical values and is often more convincing in practice than other religions, especially because of its general non-violence and its commitment to all creatures.

For the sake of completeness, Taoism, Confucianism and Shinto should also be mentioned. While Taoism and Confucianism are mainly located in China, Shinto is a religion almost exclusively confined to Japan. Unlike Taoism and Shinto, Confucianism is not a religion in the strict sense, but a pragmatic code of ethics that goes back to the doctrine of the philosopher Confucius who lived in China in about 500 B.C. Confucius taught that man must "seek harmony with the world as a whole". Similar to Hinduism, Taoism and Shinto are not homogeneous beliefs; rather they combine different early religious, essentially polytheistic ideas.

Moreover, many similarities can be observed between all religions in terms of their ethical demands. The search for the true and good, and so for the liberation from evil, is the guiding principle of all religions. Even the religious practices to achieve this goal are often similar. On the other hand, we must say that the different religious views are often contradictory, which suggests that we are also dealing here with errors. It is the task of a religious dialogue and of the further search for truth to overcome these errors. This requirement applies of course not only to the different religions, but to all worldviews and resulting ethical conceptions. The truth does not need to shy away from an honest intellectual debate, because it can only win.

The situation is different when debating with those who are not really interested in a dialogue for the sake of truth. Such discussions are mostly useless and do not help in the search for truth. On the contrary, they give rise to the risk that conflicting positions harden and that the focus is no longer on ascertaining the truth, but only on promoting one's "own thing". The people of goodwill are those on whom we must base our hope that the different paths followed in search of the one truth are not misleading, but lead to the common goal.

However, we must still deal with the claims of non-religious worldviews which unilaterally rely upon pure reason and argue that their way to search for the truth and to do what is right is the best one. Especially in the wake of the Enlightenment it became clear that religious ideas about what exists and happens in nature often were not consistent with the intellectual knowledge of that time and had to be revised. Even on the question of doing right one had to realise that misconceptions lead to wrong actions. Religion became discredited. The human mind alone seemed to be a guarantor for what is right. Politically, this revolutionary spirit emerged for the first time during the French Revolution. The positivistic thinking of this new time left no room for God and the transcendent. However, the new socio-political currents of the 19th century such as liberalism and socialism in its various forms also had a critical or hostile attitude towards religion. Scientific knowledge based on a materialistic core belief, technical progress and new forms of state societies, initially under the motto "Liberty, Equality, Fraternity", then more and more party rule, either under the ideal of freedom or of equality, were the new "ways of salvation". The increased emphasis on the state went hand in hand with the nation-state mentality. What they all had in common was the negation of an existing higher authority to which man has to subordinate himself. It was replaced by the human mind that recognised the laws of nature as given, but considered them more as things that you make subservient to yourself to create a "better world" according to one's own standards. This attitude has dominated the thinking of modern, self-determined people until our time, although the 20th century and its devastating world wars, the invention of weapons of mass destruction, the inhuman forms of rule under National Socialism and Communism and the increasing risk of man-made destruction of the environment have contributed to the fact that the unlimited faith in human reason and thus the belief in progress began to waver and a subliminal pessimism has spread. This uneasiness has been reflected most in the intellectual attitude of existentialism, which on the one hand has questioned any orientation of man towards principles of order beyond one's own existence, but on the other hand has seen hardly any way out of the dilemma of man's negative experience of the world on the basis of his own existential possibilities. Moreover, the emergence of relativistic and nihilistic attitudes, which deny any existence of recognisable, valid and therefore binding criteria of truth, reflects this development.

If we critically reconsider the different "ways of salvation" and take into account my initially made basic epistemological reflections, particularly those ways have to be described as aberrations, which regardless of a recognisable, from the existence of man independently existing reality and thus from the objective truth make human the sole standard of the "right actions". As we have bitterly experienced again and again in the history of mankind, this has mostly evil consequences. But even those who rely on "God-given or natural laws and fundamental rights" must ask themselves to what extent their often divergent or contradictory views derive from the one indivisible truth that does not allow a contradiction in terms. Is the true and good, even with direct reference to "God", not often turned into its opposite, so that evil is the result?

Where shall we go in view of all these deficiencies? I have already answered this question for myself, but I think that those who are still searching and still have to decide, in the light of what has been said, should recognise and profess that the way to overcome evil can most likely be found in Jesus Christ and his message. However, this does not mean that it is sufficient to rely upon Christ and his message to attain salvation. Jesus himself said that not everyone who says to him "Lord, Lord" shall enter into the kingdom of God, but only he who does the will of God (Matt. 7, 21). This also means that all those who try to work for the true and good are on the way to God. However, the path itself is not yet the goal and different paths does not mean that they all lead to the same goal. Therefore, in spite of our honest search for the right path, in the end it can be decisive for our salvation that we let ourselves be guided by Jesus as his followers in obedience to God, especially when following this path involves suffering.

However, the faith in Jesus Christ and his salvation path has considerable consequences. Despite the already mentioned human right to personal religious freedom and freedom of choice and thereby the tolerance towards other faiths and unbelieving seekers of truth, Jesus insists that for the realisation of the kingdom of God we follow him not half-heartedly, but with determination. Pluralism is not required; Christ requests that we freely decide to follow him. We are called upon to listen to his words and to act accordingly.

Jesus' words are handed down to us in the gospels. Even if they have not been recorded verbatim and although inaccurate translations may have caused additional changes, nevertheless, the spirit that speaks out of the words of

Jesus is unambiguous. First of all there is the demand for unconditional love of truth. This demand is identical to the requirement deduced from the purely epistemological considerations that accordance with the truth is the basic condition for everything good.

The situation becomes more difficult when Jesus demands that we believe in him. Certainly this means not only faith within the meaning of having confidence in the person of Jesus as someone who wants the best for us; Jesus' demand goes much further: He wants us to recognise him as the only saviour and redeemer of the world, who has been directly sent by God. The statement "Whoever sees me, sees the Father" (John 14, 9) and "No one comes to the Father except through me" (John 14, 6) goes so far as to say that true knowledge of God is only possible in the devotion to Jesus Christ and in listening to his message of salvation. Faith in Christ certainly also entails belief in his healings and miracles, but above all, means that we see that the only path to salvation, which can bring complete deliverance from all evil, is in the way of the cross and in the sacrificial death, which Jesus has taken upon himself in accordance with the true and good and thus in loving obedience to God. We too, when we follow Jesus in loving obedience, will share his resurrection and obtain salvation from all suffering and death. Viewed in this manner, the faith in Christ is quite a challenge, exceeding normal human capacities. But deliverance from all evil also means that normal human capacities are not enough to overcome evil. Ultimately, salvation comes from God himself. However, since our human knowledge is not sufficient to comprehend God, we depend on faith, and because Christ is credible, the belief in him is justified.

Hereinafter, I will try to evaluate the legacy of Jesus in view of its significance for salvation.

At first there is the demand of Jesus for penance and conversion. Again and again, Jesus condemns self-righteousness. Self-righteousness blocks the path to conversion, which is a prerequisite for a turn for the better. Jesus shows in many parables that a sinner who repents is closer to salvation than a "righteous one" who is of the opinion that there is no need for repentance and conversion. If we consider this basic requirement critically from the point of view of overcoming all falsity and evil, we must admit that the latter is only possible in the full realisation of the true and good, namely the total dedication to God, which also includes loving devotion to one's neighbour. If someone practices self-righteousness in the face of this requirement, he is not honest with himself, because before God we are all sinners.

Conversion of sinners and remission of sins are central aspects of salvation. Jesus' parable of the "lost son who remorsefully returns to the house of his father" also stands for the "lost creation that is returning to God with the hope of redemption".

On the other hand, the turning away from God and the search for self-realisation without referring back to him as the source of the true and good is misleading and ultimately leads to perdition. The demand for conversion and penance means therefore steady, faithful, and loving devotion to God and the waiving of all self-righteousness. In the parable of Jesus, however, the "older son" lacked the latter and hence did not have a proper relationship with his brother, about whose conversion and salvation he could not rejoice. While the sins of the "remorsefully returning son" are forgiven, the "self-righteous son" is not forgiven for his wrongness. Without insight into our own inadequacy, sin and guilt cannot be forgiven, and without forgiveness of sins salvation cannot take place. "Forgive us our trespasses, as we forgive those who trespass against us" is a petition of the Lord's Prayer which is also a prayer for salvation. Jesus himself repeatedly forgave sins and commissioned his disciples appointed by him as trustees to forgive others their guilt. Penance and forgiveness of sins are events of salvation and therefore they must form the focus of the salvific mission also for those who bear responsibility today in the succession of Jesus.

Apart from the demand for penance and forgiveness of sins Jesus left another important legacy as a healing tool on the way to salvation. He called himself the bread of life, and on the eve before his suffering he handed bread and wine to his chosen apostles with the words: "This is my body which is given for you" and "This cup is the new testament in my blood which is shed for you" (Luke 22, 19–20). The disciples celebrated this supper, the beginning of the young Christian community, in memory of Jesus in awareness of the presence of Jesus in the form of bread and wine and in memory of the words of Jesus who had said: "Whoever eats my flesh and drinks my blood has eternal life and I will raise him up on the last day" (John 6, 54).

The Lord's Supper in remembrance of the suffering and death of Jesus as the redeeming sacrifice, and with faith in the sacramental presence of Jesus in the form of bread and wine has always been the centre of Christian religious practice, but on the other hand the separation of Christians into various denominations is felt nowhere more painfully than in the termination of the table fellowship. At the Last Supper Jesus instructed his disciples to be one and to love one another so that everybody might recognise that they were his disciples. The schisms in the Christianity are therefore a nuisance, which, however, cannot only be overcome by restoring the table fellowship. Genuine altar fellowship always presupposes the inner communion with Christ and with each other. The apostle Paul admonishes the young Christian community in Corinth, which was in danger of splitting, telling them to adopt a more worthy celebration of the Lord's Supper: "Whoever eats of this bread or drinks from this cup of the Lord in an unworthy manner, will be guilty of the body and blood of the Lord. But let a man examine himself, and so let him eat of that bread and drink of that cup. For he who eats and drinks unworthily eats and drinks damnation to himself not discerning the Lord's body" (I Corinthians 11, 27–29). An essential prerequisite for the worthy celebration of the Lord's Supper is therefore the common belief in the sacramental presence of Christ in the form of bread and wine and the internal integrity of the individual. Where this is the case, the overcoming of the divisions must also be possible. This in turn is a prerequisite for the joint worthy celebration of the Lord's Supper. Because only if we as Christians have unity with each other and love one another as Christ has told us, can we with good conscience come together at his table.

Here, of course, the question arises of where, in view of the inconsistencies between the various Christian denominations, we find true Christianity. Similar to the different religions, here too, the various doctrines are largely outside a cognitive scientific verifiability. It is also true here that because of the own conviction as well as for the sake of the truth, mutual tolerance has to be demanded. Nevertheless, it must be clear that the separations of Christianity into different confessions and ecclesial communities are contrary to Jesus' demand for unity. Christ links the unity above all with the faith in his message and with the mutual love of those who rely on him. As can easily be seen, the unity in faith presupposes a uniform understanding of Jesus' message. A different understanding is not necessarily based on the lack of willingness to listen to Jesus' words, but may also be the result of misunderstandings, especially since not everything that is recorded in the gospels about Jesus and his words is entirely clear. But the spirit which speaks out of Jesus' words is, as already mentioned, unequivocal. That this divine spirit, if we open ourselves totally to it, will not mislead us, but lead us to the true and good – in this we may trust. Therefore, religious schisms are always signs of human guilt, particularly with regard to love of God and love of neighbour. Because if we as Christians loved God above all and therefore also Him who was sent to our rescue and who died for our salvation on the cross, and if we loved our neighbours as ourselves, then we would also progress on the way to the true and good and thus increasingly become one with Christ and with one another.

A visible sign of being a Christian is generally considered the baptism, which in the early church was connected with a conscious and deliberate personal commitment to Christ, to his doctrine of salvation and to the community of all the baptised. This character of a personal faith decision has been largely lost through the later generally practised infant baptism and the convention that one is, so to speak, born into a faith community. Being baptised is today far from bearing witness to Christ and his message. However, without the commitment to Christ an important prerequisite for the right to call oneself a Christian is missing. True Christianity therefore always requires faith in Christ and his message.

Accordingly, the question of where to find true Christians cannot be answered only on the basis of the formal belonging to a Christian community. True Christians are those who, as well as having received the sacrament of baptism, also personally confess Christ, believe in his message and seek to follow it. This discipleship of Christ requires above all the love of God and the love of neighbour, which find their clearest expression in the search for and realisation of the true and good, in the selfless care of others and in the search for unity of all people of good will.

The question of how one can be a true Christian is therefore less a question of denomination, but a question of an honest endeavour to follow Jesus. Of course, this also means that you have to consider the pros and cons of the various Christian denominations, and that with respect to the denominational allegiance you must follow your conscience fully focusing on the true and good.

With regard to salvation history, it should be noted that the differences and thus partly also inconsistencies of Christian confessions stand in contradiction to the salvific message, namely the realisation of the kingdom of God, in which there are no contradictions and antagonisms, but only the true and good. Therefore true Christianity also requires efforts to promote the unity of all Christians and finally of all people of good will on the basis of the true and good. After all that has been said on the issue of truth so far, it is obvious that in the search for unity the truth should not fall by the wayside.

Comparing the various Christian denominations we note that, although they all refer to Christ and his message, the different views are mostly incompatible with each other. In the search for the truth, it is therefore necessary to scrutinise the various doctrines critically. I have already emphasised that the statements of the gospels do not always provide unequivocal answers, but on the other hand, the divine spirit of the message of Jesus, which is heard in the gospels, is unambiguous. So we need to examine the confessions for compliance with this divine spirit to find ways that will bring us closer to the kingdom of God, thus overcoming all falsities and evils.

Already in early Christianity there were disagreements and the first divisions, despite the generally witnessed brotherhood among those who confessed Christ and therefore called themselves Christians. Paul exhorts the church at Corinth to be of one mind. In the fourth century, disputes about the person of Christ characterised theological thinking. During the time before the first Council of Nicaea in the year 325 and the first Council of Constantinople in the year 381 there was an ongoing dispute between the followers of the doctrine of the Trinity, which saw God as a Trinitarian consubstantial unity of Father, Son and Holy Spirit, and the so-called Arians named after one of their early representatives, Arius, which argued that the Father alone is God and Christ an image of the Father created by God. Just like the Trinitarians, the Arians also referred to the Bible. However, in the end they were in the minority, and thus in Nicaea and finally at the Council of Constantinople a binding creed was formulated for the church at that time, which is still recognised today by all Christian denominations with the exception of Jehovah's Witnesses, the Mormons and the religious communities of the Unitarians. Arianism was condemned as heresy and its followers were subjected to reprisals and persecution, just as the followers of the doctrine of the Trinity, where they were in the minority, had suffered among the Arians.

With goodwill on all sides, the great schisms in the church's history could probably have been avoided, especially since the message of Jesus and the teaching of the apostles did not give any adequate and justified reason for the later divisive conflicts. Besides the legitimate search for answers to the open religious questions the main reasons for the schisms were ecclesiastical deficiencies, diverging state-political and church-political interests, a lack of willingness for dialogue and lovelessness among those who claimed to be the true guardians and announcers of the message of Jesus and of the apostles' teaching.

Thus the separation between the Orthodox Church of the East and the Roman-Catholic Church of the West, which was accomplished by the mutual excommunication of the patriarch of Constantinople and of the Roman pope Leo IX in 1054 after centuries of estrangement, was not so much due to religious differences, but mainly a result of the political division of the former Roman Empire, with the strengthening of the papacy on the one hand and the weakening of the Byzantine Empire in the face of the spread of Islam contributing to this development.

Also in the great "Western Schism", as a consequence of which large parts of the Roman Church joined the Reformation movement of the 16th century, political reasons and especially the debate about the papacy and its claim that the bishop of Rome as successor to the apostle Peter was the sole legitimate spiritual leader of the church, played a central role. However, an additional factor triggered by the incipient Enlightenment was that also elements of the actual Christian faith and religious doctrines were generally questioned. The leading reformers, among them especially Martin Luther, declared only the Bible to be the source of true Christianity and the issue of the text interpretation was no longer a matter of the "highest teaching authority of the church"; instead, the maturity and freedom of individual Christians were emphasised .

Mutual condemnations, religious wars caused mostly by politics, Counter-Reformation efforts on the Catholic side, and fragmentation into regional and free churches on the Protestant side were consequences, which entailed serious changes in the relationship of those who continued to refer to Christ and his message. The knowledge that these divisions could not be true to the message of Jesus and could only be overcome by a common search for the right way was realised only slowly and led to today's ecumenical efforts with the objective of worldwide unification and cooperation of all Christians.

These efforts have not been without positive results, as can be seen at least in the fact that tolerance has increased among representatives of the various Christian denominations, which earlier were often fighting each other.

If we project what we have said about the conflicts between the different Christian denominations and the efforts for overcoming these contradictions onto the antagonisms between the different worldviews, we can see the problems here are of course even bigger and the search for solutions is much more difficult, because the common basis of what is considered as good and right is smaller. It is especially problematic when the opposing views, particularly regarding the crucial questions such as the responsibility of man to a higher authority existing or concerning the recognition of universal human rights and duties, which are not within the discretion of the individual or of majorities, are so polarised that common approaches in search for the true and good are very difficult to find.

Where controversies are the result of malevolence, a common basis for overcoming these antagonisms is entirely lacking. Only the conversion of those who do evil towards what is recognisable as true and good can provide a way out. As already indicated in connection with the tolerance question, for well-meaning people in this case the obligation ends to grant a malicious person the same rights as someone who feels committed to the true and good, but has a different view of what is good and right. However, we must not repay evil with evil. In this way we get ourselves into the vicious circle of evil. Jesus even calls upon us to love our enemies. This does not mean that we are called to love the evil, but that we can overcome evil only by good. "Doing good to malicious people" also does not mean that you should provide them with what is useful for their bad intentions, but what they need for salvation. On the other hand, as far as it is in our power we must guard ourselves against evil and also protect those for whom we bear responsibility.

There remains the question of how to reliably recognise real evil. As previously pointed out, not everything that contradicts the true and good and which therefore is bad is done with malicious intent. We all can make mistakes, and we are all, in our ethical behaviour, not free of weaknesses and errors. But if we love truth and goodness and seek to act upon it, we are basically of good will and not malicious. The malevolence begins where the love of the true and good does not determine our thoughts and actions, but where for the sake of "our own benefit" this is reversed into its opposite and where the resulting evil is consciously and willingly accepted.

Below I will address the issue of the origin of our world in more detail and will show that science and faith are obligated to the same indivisible truth.

In the area of science, human knowledge has rapidly developed in recent times and has in an unexpected way given us insights into the origin of the universe and our planet with its unique biosphere, which includes us as thinking human beings. Nevertheless, important questions remain unanswered from a scientific perspective.

According to the generally recognised standard model of cosmology, the beginning of our universe can be traced back to a point about 14 billion years ago. The redshift of light detected by Edwin Hubble in 1929 and reducible to a temporally expanding space made it possible to determine the start of this expansion by back-calculation. The resulting theory of a Big Bang, which assumes that the beginning of our universe was a spatio-temporal singularity, found impressive confirmation by the discovery of cosmic background radiation in 1964. The good conformance between the measured properties of the microwave background with the theoretical predictions represents an important argument for the correctness of the Big Bang theory. Accordingly, only since the Big Bang there exist space and time. Moreover, the four fundamental forces that we know today, namely gravitation, electromagnetic force, weak nuclear force and strong nuclear force revealed their effectiveness for the first time with the Big Bang. In conjunction with space and time and what fills this space in the form of visible and invisible (dark) matter and energy they build the basis for the laws of all physical events in our universe.

If this theory is correct – the high proportion of "dark matter" and "dark energy" postulated in this case as a specific cause of the observed gravitational movements of galaxies and the accelerated expansion of space is so far an unsolved scientific problem – there still remains the question about the final cause of the origin of our world. This question cannot be answered, either on the basis of the known physical laws or as a result of our logical thinking in the sense of scientific knowledge. The validity of our laws of nature has its beginning no earlier than the start of our universe. We can trace the origin of the world only to the extent that these laws, which also form the basis of our thinking, are valid. Only the step beyond that limit, namely the assumption that there is a timeless truth which is the source of all being and therefore the origin of all thinking and recognising, creates a trusting relationship to this ultimate truth, in other words makes us capable of believing in a Creator God who stands above all and from whom our present universe has evolved.

From the cosmic microwave background radiation and its redshift, i.e. the expansion of space, it is concluded that the universe must have been hotter and denser in the past. Only during its cooling were the building blocks of matter gradually formed. At a temperature of around 3,000 degrees Celsius the formation of atoms occurred, from which the first light elements, mainly hydrogen and helium, developed. Stars and galaxies did not exist at this early stage. The galaxies were formed about 1 billion years after the Big Bang from gas clouds, that is some 13 billion years ago. The cause of this was gravitation, which is effective over all distances as gravitational force of the energetic masses existing in space and thus gives shaped form to the macrocosm. The total number of galaxies observable today amounts to several hundred billion. A galaxy for its part contains up to several hundred billion stars. A star is formed when a large amount of gas (mostly hydrogen) starts to collapse as a result of gravitation. The hydrogen is heated, leading to the fusion of hydrogen atoms into helium. When the pressure of the gas and the gravity are in balance, the star remains stable in this state at a high brightness, until the nuclear fuel is exhausted. This is how our sun developed about 4.6 billion years ago from a rotating cloud of gas and the remnants of previous stars, which consisted of heavy elements. These heavy elements are formed during the explosion of a star, called a supernova. A supernova is the result of massive nuclear chain reactions occurring within a star at the end of its life. A small portion of the heavy elements formed the planets orbiting our sun. The sun loses about 14 million tonnes of hydrogen per second due to the nuclear fusion taking place in its interior. Therefore, the nuclear fuel of our sun will last for approximate five billion more years. Our sun will shrink at the end of its normal star life in about seven billion years into a white dwarf of the size of our earth.

According to today's knowledge, the universe was at least 10–12 million years old before life could originate, because life requires the formation of heavy elements. Only 20,000–40,000 light years away from the centre of the Milky Way – and this is where our solar system is located – a viable planetary area of our galaxy exists, since the heavy elements required for life occur only here.

Among all the planets which we know, only our earth verifiably offers the necessary prerequisites for the emergence of higher life. This includes in particular the existence of the basic building blocks of life, namely the elements hydrogen, oxygen, carbon, nitrogen, phosphorus and sulphur, which in turn by means of energetic processes under primeval conditions created the molecular compounds necessary for life, especially water, carbohydrates, amino acids and nucleic acids. The amino acids are for their part the building blocks of the proteins or protein compounds that exist as macromolecules and with whose help the first cells were formed under special, up to now not reproducible conditions. The self-reproducibility of these cells was the decisive step towards creating life. Thereby, the cell became the elementary basic unit of all living beings known to us. The formation of protein molecule chains can be dated to a time around four billion years ago. The fact that shortly thereafter the first cells were formed, one can conclude from the fact that the carbon C_{12}, which is only organically formed, is detectable from about 3.8 billion years. We do not know how the jump from physico-chemical to biological evolution took place. The cell is a complex compound of various proteins, carbohydrates and nucleic acids, but the most important fact is that this compound is capable of organising itself and of maintaining and reproducing itself by the "incorporation of external substances", namely by metabolism. It was also important that the cells had the ability to form cell connections and to specialise in the course of evolution. Thus, ever new organisms evolved, which during cell division transmitted their genetic information by means of the deoxyribonucleic acid (DNA). The basic building blocks of the DNA are four different types of so-called nucleotides, which consist of deoxyribose (a sugar molecule with five carbon atoms), a phosphate residue and one of four organic bases, namely adenine, cytosine, guanine or thymine. Under normal conditions, these building blocks link to form a giant molecule consisting of two nucleotide strands, the so-called double helix. The sequence of the nucleotides contains the entire genetic information, which is thus completely present in every cell of an organism.

While at the beginning of biological evolution the reproduction of single-cell and multicellular organisms took place by simple cell division, a new principle of biological reproduction, namely sexual reproduction, evolved about one billion years ago. In the case of simple cell division, there is normally no change in the genetic information of the DNA, which we call mutation. It is only by sexual reproduction that the genetic information merges, which in the form of a single (haploid) chromosome set (mixture of DNA and proteins) is stored in the sex cells of a male and a female individual of the same species, although differing with regard to their genotype, so that a new cell is formed, the so-called zygote consisting of a double (diploid) set of chromosomes, with the ability to divide. Thus, a systematic mutation of the genotype of new individuals resulted. The sexual reproduction led therefore to a considerable acceleration of evolution, i.e. to a rapidly advancing variety of forms and complexity of life on earth.

An additional acceleration of evolution took place when the living beings began to nourish themselves from other living organisms instead from the chemical constituents of their surroundings. This behaviour increased the selection pressure by creating advantages for the superior and more adapted individuals with respect to preservation and propagation of their species. Life thus organised itself into ever higher and more complex forms up to the self-conscious man.

However, at this point I must come back to my earlier critical remarks on the instinct of self-preservation and self-realisation as an essential feature of biological evolution, which is focused primarily on one's own existential advantage and the benefit of one's own group. I had interpreted the resulting "struggle for existence" and contest without respect for the welfare of other individuals and that of the whole as a contradiction to a creation which is in accordance with the divine truth. My main argument was that the discord between human beings and similarly the hostile confrontation in the animal kingdom is felt as "evil", at least by those who suffer from it. If this "struggle for existence" as a principle of evolution were objectively good, then those who claim the "right of the stronger" would be right and all those who consider it as "evil" and help the weak would be objectively wrong. However, such a conception leads to an inner contradiction, since the "struggle for existence" without regard for the welfare of other individuals and of the whole is connected with enmity, but enmity as a conflict within the true and good is a contradiction to the general consensus of truth. Besides, we know the bad consequences of such a worldview because of our historical experience.

I assume that on the basis of freedom in the course of evolution starting from object-like organisms, subject-like individuals evolved. These individuals no longer necessarily obeyed the laws of the one consistent truth, but on the basis of freedom started to act as subjects in the sense of a *self* and thus gave priority to self-preservation and self-realisation over everything else. At the latest in humans, the resulting hostile behaviour, often associated with falseness and deception, takes place consciously in the "struggle for existence", and at the latest, man also recognises the connections and negative consequences resulting from a purely self-related behaviour, which is no longer oriented towards the welfare of others and of the whole. There are many indications that in the animal kingdom, at least in the higher animals, a kind of consciousness exists meaning that animals also painfully experience this conflict between the pursuit of self-preservation and the threat to and destruction of their own existence. I am aware that the answer to the question of to what extent this conflict is based on the laws of truth or is not caused by it (and since I have related this truth to the existence of God, this means that this conflict is or is not God's will) ultimately determines the correctness of my worldview.

If what is experienced as an "evil" is willed by God, then the subjective conception of this "evil" is wrong and thus itself of evil, or if the experience-based conception of what is an "evil" is objectively correct, this "evil" cannot be willed by God, i.e. it is not a direct consequence of a true and good Creator God.

For all worldviews the answer to this question is of crucial importance. It is remarkable that especially in Buddhism the question of experience and overcoming of suffering plays a central role. As far as human beings are concerned and as already stated, the "three mental poisons", namely, "greed", "hate" and "blindness" are held responsible for the experience of suffering. A little more profound and thus not only related to humans is the statement that the "struggle for existence" is ultimately a matter of "self-assertion of an illusionary self towards the fellow beings". This, however, is exactly what has developed in the course of evolution. Buddhism sees this development as natural, but in contrast it attempts to overcome the resulting suffering through adopting a "right view" and "right action" and ultimately to replace it by an existence in "nirvana", which is free from suffering.

In Judaism, Christianity and Islam the suffering is interpreted as a result of sin, i.e. as a result of the turning away from God. But since suffering and the experience of death already existed when there were still no human beings, sin would have to be more original than man.

Detached from all philosophical-theological considerations there is no reason to assume that death, i.e. the destruction of a living organism caused by external or internal influences, is not given as a fact from the very beginning of the existence of such organisms.

Only the reproduction and thus the transmission of life in the form of the same species or of species-related new organisms enabled the survival of a species or the development of new living beings. These conditions did not change even when in the course of the long-lasting process of evolution from initially primitive, object-like organisms there evolved highly complex, subject-like living beings. What was new, however, was that these subject-like living beings obviously no longer reacted only according to given physico-chemical laws, but began to act in the sense of a *self*. Thus, these living beings came into conflict with their environment and with each other. Death was now no longer only the result of a process running according to given laws, but it was felt to be an "evil" and was combated. For the first time here a traceable contradiction arose to the fundamental, self-consistent truth, which we experience in faith also as personal God.

The question remains of whether evil based on a conscious decision was also born in this way. I indicated at the beginning that the creatures concerned can hardly be held responsible for their behaviour. Only man can consciously sin as far as we can judge this on the basis of our world of experience. Thus the "conscious evil act" is confined to man. However, this is not satisfactory in the face of the "experienced evils" which according to what has been said above are more original than man. This is because "evils" existing only on the basis of freedom, without responsibility and guilt, have a random character and call into question a God-given, good creation and thus also the existence of God.

To answer this question I come back to the statement that according to Christian-Jewish but also Islamic doctrine, in addition to God and his Spirit of Truth other spirit beings called "angels" or "demons" exist and the spirit of untruth by turning away from God exists in varied forms as a contradiction to the truth. Christ speaks of "Satan" as the adversary of God. Similar to God, within the scope of the free divine order this spirit of contradiction against the true and good can have an effect on creation, and this conscious action in the sense of what contradicts the true and good is called "evil". As far as man with his conscious and deliberate decision-making freedom is concerned, we speak of "temptation" just as we speak on the other hand of "grace", when "God's help" is given to man.

In the gospels it is reported in various passages that animals and humans were possessed by "evil spirits" and that Christ himself was led into temptation by "Satan". Today's psychology which rejects such an interpretation and attempts to explain the mentioned phenomena in a purely rational manner, ignores the fact that evil is present in a manifold, materially incomprehensible way in the world and that the destructive intention which emanates from it – we need only think of the atrocities in the recent history of mankind – eludes a purely scientific explanation. However, it is right that evil, where it has the possibility of influencing the created, also provokes pathological changes which, if not cured, will continue to foster new evil. "This is the curse of the evil deed, that it will go on begetting new evil", Octavio Piccolomini says in Friedrich Schiller's "Wallenstein". As far as man is concerned, we speak of "original sin" in this context. But it is difficult to identify where the underlying and last cause of a misdevelopment should be sought. The statement of the apostle Paul, according to which "by one man sin entered into the world, and death by sin; and so death passed upon all men, for that all have sinned" (Rom 5, 12), is based solely on the Biblical Creation Report without awareness of the real process of evolution, and therefore attributes to man the actual blame for the evil in the world that is focused on the example of the human experience of death. Compared with this, the problem of sin and its negative effects on creation become clear in the parable of Jesus "Wheat and Weed" (Matthew 13, 37–43), in which Jesus names the adversary of God, namely Satan, as mainly responsible for evil and its consequences. This parable is in line with the sequence of events that occurred in the course of evolution, and does not question the responsibility of man for his own free actions and their consequences.

After this excursion to answer the extremely difficult question of how to assess the instinct of self-preservation and self-realisation which occurs within the scope of biological evolution and largely determines the behaviour of the individuals we still have to consider the further and highly important evolutionary step from unconscious to conscious life.

The knowledge of human consciousness results solely from the experience of one's own consciousness and the analogy that other people, especially as they can communicate their own experiences and feelings through language, have a consciousness similar to ours.

On the other hand, a statement about the states of consciousness of non-human beings is hardly permissible in this way, since a direct analogy is not applicable because of the great diversity of intellectual abilities, and a judgement is largely impossible due to the lack of linguistic communication. Nevertheless, from the experience of the development of one's own consciousness in the toddler age the evolutionary development of consciousness in general may be inferred with some justification. As there is a similarity in the developmental state of human and animal intelligence, similarities are also conceivable with regard to the presence or absence of consciousness.

The earliest memories of my own conscious existence date back to my second year of life. I seem to recall that I was standing in the kitchen of my parents' house and said 'Now I am already two years old.' I also remember my rattle with which I played. This also suggests that the earliest memories go back to the age before my third year. The oldest memories are sporadic "islands of consciousness," which with progressive age occurred at ever shorter intervals. It is only from the age of five years that I can speak of a "continuous consciousness". The most important experiences of the year 1945, inter alia the bombing alarms and the escape into the cellar rooms of the parental home, the invasion of the American troops, the confiscation of the parental house, the replacement of the Americans by French occupation soldiers and my attendance at the kindergarten from the autumn of 1945 on have remained vividly in my memory until today. Consciousness is obviously tied to the ability of memory and thus to the brain's ability to memorise and recall memory contents. The fact that these memory contents become conscious, however, is quite another matter. The ability to store large amounts of data and to make them available again, when required, is something that computers have too. However, if it is claimed that computers may have consciousness, it should be realised that the interconnection of all computers of the world into a gigantic supercomputer is far from creating consciousness. Consciousness obviously presupposes more than what we can describe with physico-chemical and biological processes.

Here again the important question arises of to what extent there is also animal consciousness. In the year 2007, researchers led by Esther Herrmann of the Max Planck Institute of Evolutionary Anthropology in Leipzig tested 100 2.5-year-old children and 100 chimpanzees for their social-cognitive abilities to interpret the behaviour of the test leader, as well as the physical-cognitive efficiency – the ability to orient themselves in the environment. While the apes could compete with the children in the latter case and were even superior to them in some tasks, all the children achieved better social-cognitive performance: they completed 76 percent of the tasks successfully, the apes only 33 percent. (Specialist magazine "Science", volume 317, page 1360). An important experiment in this context is also the investigation of the ability of animals to recognise themselves in a mirror. Such experiments have been successfully carried out with apes and elephants. However, dogs, cats and other animal species, recognise in the mirror image only a relative who soon becomes uninteresting. Of course, we cannot draw any reliable conclusions about the presence or absence of consciousness among our animal relatives from such test results, especially since we know that consciousness is not a necessary prerequisite for intelligent behaviour, and there is also no explanation of how consciousness ultimately comes about. But, on the other hand, we know that man only possesses consciousness at a certain developmental stage of his brain, and our personal experience teaches us that the human ability to act intelligently and creatively also depends on the fact that our action becomes conscious and that we can reflect consciously on the results of our action. Since even highly intelligent and creative behaviour can be observed in animals, we cannot rule out the fact that there is already a kind of consciousness of the more highly developed animals. Conversely, we may also assume with some justification that in the more primitive creatures, namely those in which the formation of the brain does not allow a pronounced remembrance and self-reflection, there is no consciousness yet. However, because ultimately we do not know whether and to what extent animal consciousness exists, there result important consequences in respect of the demands on our ethical behaviour towards animals.

As we cannot exclude that animals have a kind of consciousness, we must also assume that these animals may have a feeling similar to humans about what is "good" or "bad" for them. In the case of the animals, too, such a feeling is not oriented to what is objectively true and good, but, as I have pointed out above, results from the evolutionary striving for self-preservation and species survival of the respective individuals. However, similar to a little child, animals are not yet capable of acting autonomously. Such behaviour, which is largely predetermined by innate behaviour patterns, is also known as "instinctive". It is only through man, who is able to act autonomously, that the situation of animals has also changed considerably. Man's capacity for redemption also has an effect on God's creation, and thus also on the situation of the animals, to the extent that man is capable of changing the world for the better. However, in the negative sense this also means that man, by doing evil, also affects the creation. Animals' welfare is therefore highly dependent on human behaviour. Man is thus not only responsible for himself, but also for the rest of creation. Similar to dealing with fellow human beings, it is also true that it is not one's own advantage or the advantage of the own group, but the well-being of the whole and thus also that of other living beings, that must be the measure of action. Here, however, much is far from satisfactory. Not only the ruthless exploitation and destruction of the environment, but above all the treatment of the animals, our fellow creatures, which are often treated only as "useful or harmful objects" without consideration of their own needs, shows to what extent man can deviate from what is true and good. However, the negative consequences of this acting ultimately also impact on the people themselves.

Man, as one of the latest links in the chain of evolution, cannot be seen as detached from all that was and is essential, so that life became possible, finally in its conscious form. Therefore, man also shows arrogance if he acts as if he were the real master of creation.

Looking back, the developmental history of living beings reveals that evolution is generally directed towards the increasingly developed and therefore more intelligent organisms. Since this is not only the case with the development lineage of primates, it can be speculated that with progress of evolution also other creatures, which are not part of the primate lineage, will continue to develop in the direction of higher intelligence. Hence, it cannot be excluded that consciousness can occur beyond man. The thought that everything that exists can be traced back to an original creative entity suggests in this context that what we experience as consciousness already existed as an idea at the dawn of creation. This consideration is important, since we can only explain in such a way that "evil," which presupposes conscious action in the sense of what is contrary to the true and good, is more original than man.

Since the truth itself by definition cannot be the cause of "evil", the spirit of contradiction against the true and good, which is possible due to freedom, must be responsible for it. Because responsibility presupposes conscious and deliberate action, it follows that either man, of whom we know that he can consciously and deliberately decide against the true and good, bears the sole responsibility for the "evil" in the world or that the spirit of contradiction against the true and good is more original than man and exists, only indirectly recognisable, as a being that is endowed with consciousness and free will.

The arguments that contradict the thesis that evil has come into the world only with man, I have set out several times. However, if evil is more original than man and responsibility in the sense of "guilt" cannot be attributed to animals acting instinctively, only two possible answers remain to the question of where the evil actually originated. One possible answer might be that there is no pre-human responsibility in the sense of conscious and deliberately free action, then the original creative entity is nothing more than an unconscious principle without free will, which is the basis of all being, in other words the "all-explanatory world formula", which is investigated by natural scientists and has caused "good" and "bad" from the perspective of the living beings, who unpredictably emerged and are even endowed with feeling and consciousness. Then this primal law would have caused contradictories without responsibility beyond its own rules and it would be itself the starting point of contradictories and thus within itself contradictory in the sense of the true and good. The alternative answer to this question is the view that the original creative entity is more than a "blind" and "unconscious" law of nature, i.e. "seeing" and "knowing". This entity then also "knows" the contradiction between truth and untruth, and since truth is more original than untruth, which presupposes existence of truth, it does not tolerate contradiction in itself in accordance with the truth. It is therefore of the same essence as truth and thus true and good. As we see, we are again approaching the concept of God, which, as far as it is based on pure rational factors, is not yet identical to the images of God in the religions, but as far as the monotheistic religions are concerned, does not contradict these. However, even in the latter case there remains the question of the responsibility for the evil in the world, insofar as man is not responsible for it. If we wish to explain the evil in the world, which is not man-made, and if at the same time we want to hold on to the idea of God as the true and good primal ground of all being, we cannot help but assume that evil, namely the conscious and free decision to go against the true and good, existed already, before human consciousness and human freedom of decision permitted it. If there is a true and good God, then there must also exist the adversary, namely "Satan", the spirit of untruth and thus of evil. But how should we imagine "non-human consciousness and non-human freedom of choice", since responsible and thus conscious action at least in humans always requires functioning and waking brain activity? Here we are again faced with the problem that, first of all, we do not know how consciousness comes about, and secondly, such a question, similar to other metaphysical questions, largely eludes epistemological examination and answering. Neither the question of the existence of God or of Satan, nor the question of the existence of one's own ego can be answered with the aid of human reason alone and by means of physical laws. We can only indirectly conclude that both good and evil in the world, if there is a pre-human responsibility for them, also presuppose pre-human consciousness and pre-human freedom of decision-making. Here, too, we depend on faith. Faith, however, means to trust that truth may be accessible in other ways than just by human reasoning.

At this point, however, we have to re-examine the atheist ideology, according to which the original creative entity is nothing more than a "law of nature underlying all being". As already pointed out, such a law is not, by itself, "forward-looking". Everything existing due to it has a final cause, but the goal direction is not "pre-planned". In this case, we are dealing with a "blind", partly contradictory process up to the point where the spiritual potency, which is evidently inherent in the natural law underlying all being, "awoke", i.e. when for the first time what we call "consciousness" emerged. Due to our scientific knowledge we know that certain conditions must have existed so that man with all his abilities could come into being. For instance, the natural constants in the atomic range must have definite values, so that stable atoms and molecules which in turn are prerequisites for complex biological systems can exist. With only minor deviations of these natural constants, everything we have observed in the scope of our evolution consideration as stages of development, from the formation of the atomic building blocks up to ever more complex systems, would not have been possible. No one can scientifically explain why the natural laws are as they are, so that everything accessible to our perception could arise. Even if randomness is brought into play and if we assume that our universe is only one of an infinite number of universes, and that due to chance the conditions necessary for the development of biological systems leading to humans equipped with consciousness and cognition ability are exactly fulfilled in our universe, even in this case such an answer is still unsatisfactory, since the logic underlying the recognisable laws of nature does not exclude chance, but has essentially no random character.

If we come back to the essence of being human and assume that only man has consciousness and freedom of will, we can only speak of human responsibility. As the contradictory exists outside human responsibility, it would exist in this case due to the original natural law underlying all being. Even the idea that this natural law already contains freedom does not alter the fact that freedom without responsibility has only a random character and that no responsibility can be derived from it. Therefore, the natural law underlying all being would itself be the starting point of the discord appearing in the course of the biological evolution, in which individuals do not search for consensus on universal truth, but seek their own vital advantage. Overcoming of these contradictions would only be possible if man with his cognitive ability and freedom of decision-making were the sole ruler of nature and if he had not reached fundamental limits in the search for the truth and the realisation of the good. In the case considered here, man himself has to be regarded as the product of a law that is the cause of inconsistency, and so he probably does not have the possibility to overcome by his own efforts the contradictions in himself or in his environment. The atheist has to live with the idea that the world and therefore also he himself is fundamentally contradictory, which, however, relativises any claim to truth. The atheist, just like any other person, depends on faith if he wants to give an answer to the question of the original reason for all being.

Even after Darwin and his theory of evolution, which is correct in its approach, and even in the light of all scientific knowledge, and although the search for an "all-explaining world formula" continues, we can in good conscience keep to the conviction that there is an "anticipatory", true and good primal ground, namely God, whom, as his creatures and in faith in Jesus Christ, we can call "Father" in spite of God's own transcendental reality.

The author

Winfried Schlotter was born in 1940 during the first winter of World War II in Wirges in the Westerwald region of Germany. Despite the material needs of the post-war period, he grew up safely in an environment shaped by Christian principles and close ties with his home region. After graduating from high school in Montabaur and studying telecommunications first in Darmstadt and then in Berlin, where he met his wife, he began his professional career at 'Siemens' in Munich. After a few years he moved to the Federal Office of Defense Technology and Procurement in Koblenz and worked there in the fields of telecommunications and information technology until his retirement. He is the father of a son and a daughter, and has lived since then in Hillscheid near Koblenz, very close to his ancestral home region.

novum PUBLISHER FOR NEW AUTHORS

The publisher

*Anyone who
stops improving,
has stopped
being good!*

Based on this motto, the novum publishing company is dedicated to finding new manuscripts for publishing and for supporting authors in the long term. By now, the publisher who was founded in 1997 and received numerous awards is considered to be a specialist for new authors in Germany, Austria and Switzerland.

A free, non-binding editing will be created for each new manuscript within a few weeks.

More information about the publisher and its books can be found on the internet:

www.novumpublishing.com

Score this book on our website!

www.novumpublishing.com